# 30 Days with the IRISH MYSTICS

# 30 *Days* with the IRISH MYSTICS

*by*

Thomas J. Craughwell

TAN Books
An Imprint of Saint Benedict Press, LLC
Charlotte, North Carolina

ISBN: 978-1-935302-66-7

Cover design by Caroline Kiser.

Printed and bound in the United States of America.

TAN Books
An Imprint of Saint Benedict Press, LLC
Charlotte, North Carolina
2012

# Introduction

The pagan Irish were fond of poetry and music, and after their conversion to Christianity, many Irish poets and musicians used their gifts to praise God, the Blessed Mother, and the saints.

You'll discover that the Irish style of addressing God and the saints is very personal, as if they were speaking to an Irish king or warrior. And the poetic element is striking. For example, St. Maelmuire calls God "O bright and gleaming sun," and St. Columba speaks of heaven as "the lofty, most beautiful haven of life."

The Irish love of poetry led naturally to a love of books and learning. They collected libraries of Irish poems, legends, and historical works, and added Christian texts as well as the works of the ancient Greek and Roman authors. Isolated at the edge of Western Europe, far removed from the barbarian nations that were ransacking the Roman Empire, Ireland became a center of Celtic, Greco-

Roman, and Christian culture. It was a rare monastery or convent that did not have a school, a library, and a scriptorium where books were copied. This led to the classic description of Ireland as "the Isle of Saints and Scholars."

This 30 Days booklet introduces you to the poetic, intensely personal prayers, hymns, and meditations of the Irish mystics. Since most of these saints will be unfamiliar to most readers, we have included an appendix with capsule biographies of the saints quoted here.

May all the mystic saints of Ireland pray for you and inspire you to grow in love for Almighty God, Our Blessed Lady, and all the saints.

# 30 *Days* with
## *the* IRISH MYSTICS

## ✿✿✿ **DAY 1** ✿✿✿✿✿✿✿✿✿✿✿✿✿✿✿✿✿✿

## *The First Step*

I arise today
Through the strength of the love of cherubim,
In obedience of angels,
In service of archangels,
In the hope of resurrection to meet with reward,
In the prayers of patriarchs,
In preachings of the apostles,
In faiths of confessors,
In innocence of virgins,
In deeds of righteous men.

ST. PATRICK (C. 387–C. 464)

*For he will give his angels charge of you, to guard*
*you in all your ways. On their hands they will bear*
*you up, lest you dash your foot against a stone.*

PSALM 91:11–12

## Today's Meditation

You are never alone. God pours out his love and grace upon you every moment of your life. He has assigned a guardian angel to watch over you. He hears the prayers that the saints offer up on your behalf. Today make a conscious effort to put aside the busyness and anxieties of daily life and with true gratitude consider all the blessings you enjoy, all of which are signs of God's loving care for you.

## Prayer

*Good Lord, the saints and angels stand around your throne praising you eternally, yet so many days go by when I forget to thank you for the blessings you shower upon me. As I begin these thirty days of prayer and meditation, clear my mind of distractions, touch my heart with your love, and draw me closer to you.*

*St. Patrick, and all you mystic saints of Ireland, pray for me!*

## ✠✠✠ DAY 2 ✠✠✠✠✠✠✠✠✠✠✠✠✠✠✠✠✠✠

### *Pleasing God*

Three things that please God most are true faith in God with a pure heart, a simple life with a grateful spirit, and generosity inspired by charity. The three things that most displease God are a mouth that hates people, a heart harboring resentments, and confidence in wealth.

ST. ITA (DIED C. 570)

*What does it profit, my brethren, if a man says he has faith but has not works? Can his faith save him? If a brother or sister is ill-clad and in lack of daily food, and one of you says to them, "Go in peace, be warmed and filled," without giving them the things needed for the body, what does it profit? So faith by itself, if it has no works, is dead.*

JAMES 2:14–17

## Today's Meditation

Just as God is merciful and generous to you, be generous to others. Flip through your checkbook—how often this year have you given to charities? Your gift doesn't have to be a small fortune—the widow's mite was more pleasing to Jesus than the bags of surplus gold the rich men gave. Now that you've examined your checkbook, examine your conscience: root out any grudges you've been nursing. The good works God expects from us are not just donations, but also good will toward our neighbors.

## Prayer

*Father, remove from my heart all feelings of bitterness and resentment. Help me to be a peacemaker in my home, my workplace, my community. Teach me to be generous and always ready to do good, no matter how small that good work may be.*

*St. Ita, and all you mystic saints of Ireland, pray for me!*

✤✤✤ **DAY 3** ✤✤✤✤✤✤✤✤✤✤✤✤✤✤✤✤✤✤✤✤

## *The Happy Family*

God, protect the house, and the household,
God, consecrate the children of the motherhood,
God, encompass the flocks and the young;
Be Thou after them and tending them

ANONYMOUS, BLESSING OF THE HOUSE

*Your wife will be like a fruitful vine within your
house; your children will be like olive shoots
around your table.*
*Lo, thus shall the man be blessed who fears the Lord.*
*The Lord bless you from Zion! May you see the pros-
perity of Jerusalem all the days of your life!*
*May you see your children's children!*

PSALM 128:3-6

## Today's Meditation

Is there any greater joy on earth than a happy family? Savor the happy times—the arrival of children and grandchildren, the First Holy Communions and weddings, the holidays, the outings, the family meals. And give thanks to God for all of them.

## Prayer

*Almighty Father, I thank you for placing me in a loving family. Bless my family and relatives with good health, long life, happiness, and prosperity. Keep us all faithful to you, and unite us all around your throne.*

*All you mystic saints of Ireland, pray for me!*

## The Mystery of the Mass

Come all ye holy,
Take the body of your Lord,
Drink of his chalice,
Take the blood for you outpoured.

> ST. SECHNALL (DIED C. 457),
> "SANCTI VENITE" ("COME ALL YE HOLY"),
> TRANSLATED BY ADRIAN FORTESCUE

*I am the living bread which came down from heaven;
if any one eats of this bread, he will live for ever; and
the bread which I shall give for the life of the world
is my flesh.*

> JOHN 6:51

## Today's Meditation

When Jesus Christ came into the world he did so many extraordinary things: he healed the rift original sin had caused between God and man; he established the Church to show all the world and all generations the way to salvation; and he left us himself in the Eucharist, the Blessed Sacrament of the altar, so that he would always physically be present among us and our souls would receive the spiritual food they need.

## Prayer

*Good Jesus, ever present in the Blessed Sacrament, I kneel in awe before you, hidden in the forms of bread and wine. May I never be bored or distracted at Mass. May I never receive Holy Communion unworthily. And may I always be conscious that each Mass is a foretaste of the glorious liturgy celebrated by all the saints in heaven.*

*St. Sechnall, and all you mystic saints of Ireland, pray for me!*

## *Guard My Tongue*

Guard my eyes for me, Jesus son of Mary, lest
   seeing another's wealth make me covetous.
Guard for me my ears, lest they hearken to slander, lest they listen constantly to folly in the
   sinful world.
Guard for me my tongue, that I slander no man,
   that I revile no one, that I curse no one.
Guard for me my heart, O Christ, in thy love, lest
   I ponder wretchedly the desire of any iniquity.

ST. MAELMUIRE (DIED C. 1167), "LORD GUARD ME"

*I said, "I will guard my ways, that I may not sin with
my tongue."*

PSALM 39:1

## Today's Meditation

The five senses are among God's most generous gifts to us. But the Evil One, who never tires of finding ways to trip us up, tries to hijack our senses to lead us into sin. The tongue seems to be his favorite weapon, since it can cause more pain to others than any other of the senses. It can be so satisfying to unleash some cutting remark, but it will be easier to control your tongue if you recall what it feels like to be on the receiving end.

## Prayer

*Give me self-control, O God, so that I will not shame, or wound, or belittle any of your children. And if anyone shames, or wounds, or belittles me, give me the strength not to respond in kind.*

*St. Maelmuire, and all you mystic saints of Ireland, pray for me!*

## ✤✤✤ DAY 6 ✤✤✤✤✤✤✤✤✤✤✤✤✤✤✤✤✤✤✤✤✤

# The Light of the World

O Lord, grant us that love which can never die, which will enkindle our lamps but not extinguish them, so that they may shine in us and bring light to others. Most dear Savior, enkindle our lamps that they may shine forever in your temple. May we receive unquenchable light from you so that our darkness will be illuminated and the darkness of the world will be made less. Amen.

ST. COLUMBA (521–597)

*You are the light of the world. A city set on a hill cannot be hid. Nor do men light a lamp and put it under a bushel, but on a stand, and it gives light to all in the house. Let your light so shine before men, that they may see your good works and give glory to your Father who is in heaven.*

MATTHEW 5:14–16

✤✤✤ 18 ✤✤✤✤✤✤✤✤✤✤✤✤✤✤✤✤✤✤✤✤✤✤

## Today's Meditation

"You are the light of the world." What a lovely metaphor for Christians dwelling in a non-Christian, sometimes even anti-Christian, society. How are we to show our light? Through good works, Christ tells us. Everyday, do what good you can, and do it quietly. Never look for applause or attention—it is more than enough that God sees what you're doing. Every time you do good for another, the light shines a bit stronger.

## Prayer

*Lord Jesus Christ, you are the light of my life. For love of you, I want to share that light in a world that sometimes seems to be increasingly gloomy. Let there never be a day when I have not tried to push back the darkness and make the world a little brighter.*

*St. Columba, and all you mystic saints of Ireland, pray for me!*

## ✣✣✣ DAY 7 ✣✣✣✣✣✣✣✣✣✣✣✣✣✣✣✣✣✣✣✣✣

### Shielded by the Saints

Grant to us, Thou Savior of Glory,
The fear of God, the love of God, and His
    affection,
And the will of God to do on earth at all times
As angels and saints do in heaven;
Each day and night give us Thy peace.
Each day and night give us Thy peace.

ANONYMOUS, A PRAYER FOR GRACE

*Thy kingdom come, thy will be done on earth as it
is in heaven.*

MATTHEW 6:10

## Today's Meditation

A Christian is expected to submit his or her will—meaning wants and desires—to the will of God. It isn't easy. One of the consequences of original sin is our stubborn, demanding willfulness. But those who strive to submit to the will of God find that their faith in Him is greatly strengthened. And they acquire another virtue, too: humility.

## Prayer

*Lord, with St. Ignatius Loyola I pray, "Receive my entire liberty, my memory, my understanding and my whole will." Give me your grace so that each day I will become more obedient to your will. And in those difficult moments when I find it hard to submit, may the angels and saints who do your will in heaven inspire and console me.*

*All you mystic saints of Ireland, pray for me!*

## *Shielded by the Saints*

May Jesus with his apostles be our aid against
   danger.
Let Mary and Joseph cherish us, and the spirit of
   Stephen:
From every peril may the commemoration of
   Ignatius' name deliver us.
Every martyr, every hermit, every saint who lived
   in chastity,
May they be a shield to us to protect us, be an
   arrow from us against demons.

ST. COLMAN OF CLOYNE (522–C. 600)

*Be strong in the Lord and in the strength of his
might. Put on the whole armor of God, that you may
be able to stand against the wiles of the devil. . . .
Stand therefore, having girded your loins with truth,
and having put on the breastplate of righteousness,*

*and having shod your feet with the equipment of the gospel of peace; besides all these, taking the shield of faith, with which you can quench all the flaming darts of the evil one. And take the helmet of salvation, and the sword of the Spirit, which is the word of God.*

EPHESIANS 6:10–11, 14–17

## TODAY'S MEDITATION

In times of trouble it was the custom among the Irish to call upon the help of as many saints as they could think of. They looked upon the kingdom of heaven as the home of a vast and powerful army, ready to protect Christians from all harm, especially from the wiles of the Evil One. Follow the example of the Irish and call upon the saints to help you in all your trials.

## PRAYER

*Come to my aid, all you saints of heaven! Stand between me and all evil. Shield my family and friends and benefactors from all harm. And inspire us to follow your example so that we may all be united together with you in heaven.*

*St. Colman of Cloyne, and all you mystic saints of Ireland, pray for me!*

## ✥✥✥ DAY 9 ✥✥✥✥✥✥✥✥✥✥✥✥✥✥✥✥✥✥✥

### *Christ's Death and Resurrection Brings Eternal Life*

Although Jesus was crucified,
Our Lord, our Champion,
He has arisen as the pure King
Of all that he created.

> ST. AENGUS THE CULDEE, (DIED C. 830),
> THE MARTYROLOGY OF AENGUS THE CULDEE

*Do not be afraid; for I know that you seek Jesus who was crucified. He is not here; for he has risen, as he said. Come, see the place where he lay. Then go quickly and tell his disciples that he has risen from the dead.*

> MATTHEW 28:5–7

## Today's Meditation

After Christ's Passion comes his Resurrection. This is more than a historical fact, it is a promise of our future from God Himself: after death comes eternal life. As long as we are faithful to God, we have nothing to fear.

## Prayer

*God and Father, on the Cross, Christ Your Son washed away the sins of the world. It is an inestimable gift. Inspire me to live my daily life true to the teachings of Jesus Christ. Make me generous and joyful. And transform my faith from something I profess to something that I live.*

*St. Aengus and all you mystic saints of Ireland, pray for me!*

## ✥✥✥ DAY 10 ✥✥✥✥✥✥✥✥✥✥✥✥✥✥✥✥✥

### *God's Protection*

God's blessing bear us and succor us!
May Mary's Son protect us!
Under His protection may we be tonight, whither-
   soever we go, may He protect us.
In rest or in activity, seated or standing, may
   Heaven's King, shield us against every battle—
   this is the supplication we make.

ST. COLMAN (522–C. 600),
*"SEN DÉ"* (GOD'S BLESSING)

*Let the heavens praise thy wonders, O Lord, thy*
*faithfulness in the assembly of the holy ones!*
*For who in the skies can be compared to the Lord?*
*Who among the heavenly beings is like the Lord.*

PSALM 89: 5-6

## TODAY'S MEDITATION

"Nothing is impossible with God." We all know this saying, yet do *you* believe it? Do you truly trust your life, your future, to Almighty God? St. Colman reminds us that in every battle, that is to say, every struggle of our life—our family, career, health, finances—we must place ourselves under the protection of God our Father.

## PRAYER

*Almighty God, the eternal protector of all humankind, shield me from everything that may weaken my faith or draw me away from your love. Strengthen me with your grace so that I can meet the challenges that seem to come every day and help me resist the temptations that seem to come every hour.*

*St. Colman, and all you mystic saints of Ireland, pray for me!*

## ❧❧❧ DAY 11 ❧❧❧❧❧❧❧❧❧❧❧❧❧❧❧❧

## *Ambassadors for Christ*

Christ with me, Christ before me, Christ behind
me,
Christ in me, Christ beneath me, Christ above me,
Christ on my right, Christ on my left,
Christ when I lie down, Christ when I sit down,

ST. PATRICK, "THE LORICA," OR BREASTPLATE

*We are ambassadors for Christ, God making his
appeal through us.*

2 CORINTHIANS 5:20

## Today's Meditation

Before he ascended into heaven, the Risen Christ said, "Go forth and teach all nations." At that particular moment he was addressing his mother Mary and his disciples, but as with everything Our Lord said, he was also addressing all Christians down through the ages. You may not have the call to be a missionary, but by practicing the virtues you can be an ambassador for Christ to everyone you meet.

## Prayer

*Lord Jesus Christ, I cannot live without you. Let my love for you grow each day, and let me translate that love into good works.*

*St. Patrick, and all you mystic saints of Ireland, pray for me!*

## *Hail Mary!*

Hail, Mary! Hail, Mary!
Queen of grace, Mother of mercy;
Hail, Mary, in manner surpassing,
Fount of our health, source of our joy.

Bestow upon us, thou Root of gladness,
Since thou art the cup of generous graces,
The faith of John, and Peter, and Paul.

ANONYMOUS, "HAIL, MARY"

*My soul magnifies the Lord, and my spirit rejoices in
God my Savior, for he has regarded the low estate of
his handmaiden. For behold, henceforth all generations will call me blessed; for he who is mighty has
done great things for me, and holy is his name.*

LUKE 1:46–49

## Today's Meditation

More than two thousand years ago the Archangel Gabriel greeted Mary as "full of grace." We know the tremendous graces God bestowed on Our Lady: her preservation from all stain of original sin; her perpetual virginity; her assumption, body and soul, into heaven. But if Mary is a marvel, she is also a mother who loves us, and cares for us, and is always ready to help us.

## Prayer

*Holy Mary, Mother of God, ever since I was a small child I have loved you above every saint in heaven. Watch over me and all my family, friends, and benefactors. Protect us with your prayers, console us with your compassion, and lead us all to your Son so that forever we may join you and magnify the Lord.*

*Holy Mother of God, and all you mystic saints of Ireland, pray for me!*

# ❖❖❖ DAY 13 ❖❖❖❖❖❖❖❖❖❖❖❖❖❖❖❖❖

## *Make Haste to Help Me*

My God, help me. Give me love of thee, O Son of my God. Glorious King, swiftly bring love of thee into my heart that it may be whole. Lord, give what I ask of thee—give, give speedily, O bright and gleaming sun.

ST. MAELMUIRE (DIED C. 1167),
"DEUS MEUS ADIUVA ME" ("MY GOD HELP ME")

*Be pleased, O God, to deliver me! O Lord, make haste to help me! . . . May all who seek thee rejoice and be glad in thee! May those who love thy salvation say evermore, "God is great!"*

PSALM 70:1, 4

## Today's Meditation

There is no darkness that the light of the Lord cannot dispel. There is no danger that the power of God cannot drive away.

## Prayer

*My God, I ask you for so many things—help with my family and my work, good health, relief from financial anxieties. Today I ask you to fill my heart with love for you.*

*St. Maelmuire, and all you mystic saints of Ireland, pray for me!*

菱菱菱 **DAY 14** 菱菱菱菱菱菱菱菱菱菱菱菱菱菱菱菱菱菱菱菱菱

## Christ's Yoke

O helper of workers . . .
I beg that I, a little man
trembling and most wretched,
rowing through the infinite storm of this age,
may be drawn by Christ to the lofty,
most beautiful haven of life.

ST. COLUMBA (C. 521–597)

*Come to me, all who labor and are heavy laden, and I will give you rest. Take my yoke upon you, and learn from me; for I am gentle and lowly in heart, and you will find rest for your souls. For my yoke is easy, and my burden is light.*

MATTHEW 11: 28-30

## Today's Meditation

In a busy week, religious obligations can sometimes seem to be just one more onerous, time-
consuming duty. But perform them anyway.
Mass on Sundays and holy days (and maybe
a bit more frequently, when possible), daily
prayer, fasting and abstinence, acts of charity;
all combine to change you for the better. The
change may be imperceptible day to day, but
over time the difference will be dramatic.

## Prayer

*Renew my fervor and devotion, O Lord, so that
I let nothing distract me from loving and serving you.*

*St. Columba, and all you mystic saints of Ire-
land, pray for me!*

## ❖❖❖ DAY 15 ❖❖❖❖❖❖❖❖❖❖❖❖❖❖❖

### *The Liturgy in Heaven*

O Christ my beloved,
O Christ of the Holy Blood,
By day and by night
I praise Thee.

ANONYMOUS, "THE LIGHTENER OF THE STARS"

*Worthy is the Lamb who was slain, to receive power and wealth and wisdom and might and honor and glory and blessing! And I heard every creature in heaven and on earth and under the earth and in the sea, and all therein, saying, "To him who sits upon the throne and to the Lamb be blessing and honor and glory and might for ever and ever!"*

REVELATION 5:12–13

## Today's Meditation

The fourth and fifth chapters of the Book of Revelation describe the liturgy in heaven, where all the angels and saints praise Christ, the Lamb of God, without ceasing. Throughout the day, and even if you awaken in the middle of the night, make a small act of praise and adoration.

## Prayer

*My Lord and My God, I praise and adore you! I do not have the words to express my love and gratitude to you, the source of all my joys and my consolation in all my troubles. Keep me faithful to you, Lord, so that someday I may sing your praise eternally with all the angels and saints.*

*All you mystic saints of Ireland, pray for me!*

## *The Pure in Heart*

Come, who with pure hearts
In the Savior's word believe;
Come, and partaking
Saving grace from him receive.

ST. SECHNALL (DIED C. 457),
"*SANCTI VENITE*" ("COME ALL YE HOLY"),
TRANSLATED BY ADRIAN FORTESCUE

*Blessed are the pure in heart, for they shall see God.*

MATTHEW 5:8

## Today's Meditation

Who are the pure in heart? They are free from mortal sin, they are at peace with their neighbor, they seek to love and serve God above all things. Let us resolve to put God before everything, that we might be pure of heart and always keep Him in our sight.

## Prayer

*Accept my heart and all my love, O Lord. Give me your grace so I can make my heart a worthy dwelling place for you. Help me to turn away from temptations, and teach me patience when confronted with people I find disagreeable.*

*St. Sechnall, and all you mystic saints of Ireland, pray for me!*

# ❖❖❖ DAY 17 ❖❖❖❖❖❖❖❖❖❖❖❖❖❖❖❖

## *The Spirit of the Lord Is Upon Me*

May the Holy Spirit shower his blessings on us.
May Christ save us.
May He bless us.
May those saints in Heaven whose memory we
celebrate on Earth, pray for us, that, through the
invocation of thy holy name, O Jesus, our crimes
may be cancelled. Amen.

> ST. COLMAN (522–C. 600),
> "SEN DÉ" (GOD'S BLESSING)

*The Spirit of the Lord is upon me, because he has
anointed me to preach good news to the poor. He
has sent me to proclaim release to the captives and
recovering of sight to the blind, to set at liberty those
who are oppressed, to proclaim the acceptable year
of the Lord.*

LUKE 4:18–19

## Today's Meditation

When God made a covenant with Abraham, he made the patriarch's descendants his chosen people, and promised them a Messiah, a savior. When Christ the Savior came into the world, he extended the promise of salvation to all people. And so the Holy Spirit showers his graces upon all the world. This is dramatically illustrated in the liturgical calendar, which lists saints from every corner of the globe. Let us strive to one day be included in that holy canon of those blessed and saved by Christ through the many gifts and graces of the Holy Spirit.

## Prayer

*Lord God, you are glorified in your saints. Teach me to love and venerate those holy men, women, and even children who were so devoted to you, and give me the grace to imitate them.*

*St. Colman, and all you mystic saints of Ireland, pray for me!*

## Dwelling in Safety

Thanks be to Thee, Jesus Christ,
Who brought'st me up from last night,
To the gladsome light of this day,
To win everlasting life for my soul.

ANONYMOUS, MORNING PRAYER

*In peace I will both lie down and sleep; for thou
alone, O Lord, makest me dwell in safety.*

PSALM 4:8

## Today's Meditation

Every day, and every moment of every day, is a gift from God. Do not squander these gifts, but each day spend some time in prayer and perform some good work for your neighbor. In this way you will gradually grow in holiness.

## Prayer

*Loving Lord Jesus, for all your blessings I give you profound thanks. I thank you now for all those times in my life when you were gracious to me but I forgot to express my gratitude to you. Guide me each day, shield me each night, and fill my heart with love for you.*

*All you mystic saints of Ireland, pray for me!*

## *St. Michael the Archangel*

Angel! Great-miracled Michael, carry my request
to the Lord.

Ask of the forgiving God forgiveness for all my
great sins.

Do not delay! Carry my urgent request to the
King, to the High King.

Bring help, bring protection to my soul in its hour
of leaving earth.

To meet my waiting soul come stoutly with many
thousands of angels.

ST. MAELMUIRE (DIED C. 1167),<br>
PRAYER TO ST. MICHAEL

*Now war arose in heaven, Michael and his angels*
*fighting against the dragon; and the dragon and his*
*angels fought, but they were defeated and there was*
*no longer any place for them in heaven. And the*
*great dragon was thrown down, that ancient serpent,*

*who is called the Devil and Satan, the deceiver of the whole world—he was thrown down to the earth, and his angels were thrown down with him. And I heard a loud voice in heaven, saying, "Now the salvation and the power and the kingdom of our God and the authority of his Christ have come."*

REVELATION 12:7–10

## Today's Meditation

Since the first days of the Church, Christians have venerated St. Michael the Archangel as the defender of God's people against the Devil. Let us, too, seek his intercession and protection as we do battle daily with sin and temptation.

## Prayer

*St. Michael the Archangel, defend us in battle! Be our protection against the wickedness and snares of the Devil. May God rebuke him, we humbly pray. And do thou, O Prince of the Heavenly Host, by the power of God, cast into Hell, Satan, and all the other evil spirits, who wander about the world, seeking the destruction of souls.*

*St. Maelmuire, and all you mystic saints of Ireland, pray for me!*

## ❧❧❧ **DAY 20** ❧❧❧❧❧❧❧❧❧❧❧❧❧❧❧❧

### *The Sun of Righteousness*

O Lord, grant us that love which can never die, which will enkindle our lamps but not extinguish them, so that they may shine in us and bring light to others. Most dear Savior, enkindle our lamps that they may shine forever in your temple. May we receive unquenchable light from you so that our darkness will be illuminated and the darkness of the world will be made less. Amen.

ST. COLUMBA (521–597)

*You are the light of the world. A city set on a hill cannot be hid. Nor do men light a lamp and put it under a bushel, but on a stand, and it gives light to all in the house. Let your light so shine before men, that they may see your good works and give glory to your Father who is in heaven.*

MATTHEW 5:14–16

## Today's Meditation

One of Christ's most ancient titles is "the Sun of Righteousness." Like the dawn that dispels the darkness of night, he drove away sin, death, and the Devil. Then he called upon everyone—even you and me—who believed in him and loves him to carry the light of the gospel to those who are still sitting in darkness.

## Prayer

*Lord Christ, help me to diminish some of the darkness of this world with your light. Let me be worthy to be called your disciple. Let me set a good example as I go about my work every day. And let your light increase and spread, O Lord, so that more and more souls acknowledge you as their Savior.*

*St. Columba, and all you mystic saints of Ireland, pray for me!*

## *The Good Shepherd*

I arise today
Through God's strength to pilot me;
God's might to uphold me,
God's wisdom to guide me,
God's eye to look before me,
God's ear to hear me,
God's word to speak for me,

ST. PATRICK, "THE LORICA," OR BREASTPLATE

*I am the good shepherd; I know my own and my own know me, as the Father knows me and I know the Father; and I lay down my life for the sheep. And I have other sheep that are not of this fold; I must bring them also, and they will heed my voice. So there shall be one flock, one shepherd.*

JOHN 10:14–16

## Today's Meditation

Fifth-century Ireland could be a dangerous, violent place, so St. Patrick's invocation of God's strength was no poetic flourish. Our own society is becoming increasingly hostile to religious believers, which makes our reliance on Christ, the Good Shepherd more vital than ever.

## Prayer

*Be my ruler and guide, good Lord, today and all the days of my life. Direct me along the path that leads to eternal life, and keep me safe from all the dangers of this world.*

*St. Patrick, and all you mystic saints of Ireland, pray for me!*

## ❖❖❖ DAY 22 ❖❖❖❖❖❖❖❖❖❖❖❖❖❖❖❖❖

### *Love Your Brother*

Let our will be firm,
Let us strive after what is dearer,
Since 'tis this that is nobler,
Let us all love Jesus!

ST. AENGUS THE CULDEE

*We love, because he first loved us. If any one says,
"I love God," and hates his brother, he is a liar; for
he who does not love his brother whom he has seen,
cannot love God whom he has not seen. And this
commandment we have from him, that he who loves
God should love his brother also.*

1 JOHN 4:19–21

## TODAY'S MEDITATION

Let go of resentments, grudges, and bitterness by praying for those who hurt you. It may be difficult to do at first, but keep trying and eventually your feelings of rancor will vanish. To love Jesus, we must give up the ill will we hold against our neighbor.

## PRAYER

*Good Jesus, with my whole heart I forgive anyone who has hurt me, and I pray for their welfare and salvation. Teach me patience when others are unkind or unjust, and keep me from treating others that way.*

*St. Aengus, and all you mystic saints of Ireland, pray for me!*

## ❁❁❁ DAY 23 ❁❁❁❁❁❁❁❁❁❁❁❁❁❁❁❁❁❁

### *The Bread of Heaven*

He to the hungry gives as food this heavenly
   bread,
Fountain of life, He gives to drink the blood
   He shed.

Christ, the source of all things, who here feeds
   us sinful men,
When this great day dawns, judge of all, will
   come again.

—ST. SECHNALL (D 457),
"SANCTI VENITE" (COME ALL YE HOLY),
TRANSLATED BY ADRIAN FORTESCUE

*The eyes of all look to thee, and thou givest them
their food in due season.*
*Thou openest thy hand, thou satisfiest the desire of
every living thing.*

PSALM 145:15–16

## Today's Meditation

Of all the gifts Christ gave us, the Blessed Sacrament is especially precious. He dwells—Body and Blood, Soul and Divinity—in every tabernacle of every Catholic church around the globe. We can go and speak with him every day. If we are in a state of grace, we can receive him every day. Have you truly considered how awe-inspiring is this gift?

## Prayer

*O God, under a marvelous sacrament you have left us the memorial of your Passion. Grant us, we beseech you, so to venerate the sacred mysteries of Your Body and Blood, that we may ever perceive within us the fruit of your Redemption. Amen.*

*St. Sechnall, and all you mystic saints of Ireland, pray for me!*

## *A Foretaste of Heaven*

Not more numerous the radiant stars which appear in the skies; not more numerous the words [of praise] which his clergy read for Christ; not more numerous the small streams which flow into the great sea, than the praises unceasing of the divine, blessed Body of Christ.

ABBOT DONOGH MÓR O'DALY (12TH CENTURY),
"IN PRAISE OF THE BLESSED EUCHARIST"

*I am the bread of life; he who comes to me shall not hunger, and he who believes in me shall never thirst.*

JOHN 6:35

## Today's Meditation

Earthly bread nourishes the body, but the Bread which came down from heaven nourishes the soul and prepares it for eternal life. The more frequently we receive Holy Communion, the more graces we receive, the closer we draw to Christ, and the further away we are drawn from the power of the Evil One.

## Prayer

*Every time I receive you in Holy Communion, good Jesus, I enjoy a foretaste of heaven, where I shall never be parted from you. May I never consciously receive you unworthily.*

*Abbot Donogh Mór O'Daly, and all you mystic saints of Ireland, pray for me!*

## DAY 25

## *The Joy of Christ*

I would like the angels of Heaven to be among us.
I would like an abundance of peace.
I would like full vessels of charity.
I would like rich treasures of mercy.
I would like cheerfulness to preside over all.

ST. BRIGID (C. 450–525)

*Love is patient and kind; love is not jealous or boastful; it is not arrogant or rude. Love does not insist on its own way; it is not irritable or resentful; it does not rejoice at wrong, but rejoices in the right. Love bears all things, believes all things, hopes all things, endures all things. Love never ends.*

1 CORINTHIANS 3:4–8

## Today's Meditation

Let your faith fill you with joy and gratitude. When you think of the mystery of the Incarnation, of the Second Person of the Holy Trinity coming to earth, taking on human flesh, and dwelling among us, how can you not feel joyful? Even the sorrow of Christ's death on the cross is tempered by feelings of awe—that our sins have been forgiven, that the gates of heaven stand open to receive us, that Christ is risen from the dead.

## Prayer

*Loving Lord Jesus, fill my heart with true affection for you and profound gratitude for your goodness. Increase my love for my neighbor and help me to dispel some of the pain and unhappiness that afflicts this world.*

## *Pray for Priests*

O holy St. Brigid, thou who art the light, the ornament, and the glory of the Church of Ireland, be the heavenly patron of its people, and be the especial friend and the protectress of the priests of the sanctuary. Let those who offer sacrifice to the name of God, be worthy of their exalted duties. Show forth in their lives the form of all perfection and cover them with the robe of holiness. Let them love justice and hate iniquity. Let their prayer be like incense in the sight of heaven. Let their doctrine be saving and salutary to the people, and let the odor of their lives be the delight of the Church of God.

ANONYMOUS, 19TH-CENTURY,
"A PRAYER TO ST. BRIGID FOR PRIESTS"

*For it was fitting that we should have such a high priest, holy, blameless, unstained, separated from sinners, exalted above the heavens. He has no need, like those high priests, to offer sacrifices daily, first for his own sins and then for those of the people; he did this once for all when he offered up himself.*

HEBREWS 7:26–27

## Today's Meditation

When was the last time you prayed for your parish priests? They have consecrated their entire lives to God to show us the way to Heaven. In spite of the scorn, ridicule, and suspicion they suffer from elements of secular society, these good men persevere in preaching the message of Jesus Christ and attempting to live it in their day-to-day lives. Years ago it was a common custom in Catholic parishes for a penitent to say a prayer for the priest who had just heard his or her Confession. That is a tradition that deserves a revival.

## Prayer

*Almighty Father, grant holiness, fervor, courage, wisdom, and charity to the men you called to serve you as priests and to the seminarians who are preparing for the priesthood. Send to your Church many more men who love you and long to save souls.*

## *The Beautiful Mystery of the Holy Trinity*

Let each man then who wishes to be saved believe first in God the first and last, one and three, one in substance, three in character; one in power, three in person; one in nature, three in name; one in Godhead, Who is Father and Son and Holy Spirit, one God, wholly invisible, inconceivable, unspeakable, Whose property it is ever to exist since God the Trinity is eternal.

ST. COLUMBANUS,
"SERMON FOR TRINITY SUNDAY"

*O the depth of the riches and wisdom and knowledge of God! How unsearchable are his judgments and how inscrutable his ways! "For who has known the mind of the Lord, or who has been his counselor?" "Or who has given a gift to him that he might be*

*repaid?" For from him and through him and to him*
*are all things. To him be glory for ever. Amen.*

ROMANS 11:33–36

## TODAY'S MEDITATION

We were baptized in the name of the Holy Trinity. We begin and end our prayers invoking the Holy Trinity. We are blessed and absolved in the name of the Holy Trinity. These actions demonstrate that although no one can fully grasp this mystery, it is essential to our faith.

## PRAYER

*Triune God, Father, Son, and Holy Spirit, our minds cannot grasp the mystery of the Holy Trinity, yet we profess our faith in it because you have revealed this truth to us. Keep us constant in the faith we have received from you, so at the end of our days here on earth, we may see your glory and praise you forever.*

*St. Columbanus, and all you mystic saints of Ireland, pray for me!*

## ✦✦✦ DAY 28 ✦✦✦✦✦✦✦✦✦✦✦✦✦✦

### *Mary's Never Dying Fame*

In alternate measure chanting,
Daily sing we Mary's praise,
And, in strains of glad rejoicing,
To the Lord our voices raise.

With a two-fold choir repeating
Mary's never dying fame,
Let each ear the praises gather,
Which our grateful tongues proclaim.

Judah's ever-glorious daughter,
Chosen mother of the Lord,
Who, to weak and fallen manhood
All its ancient worth restored.

ST. CUCHUMNEUS (DIED 745),
"HYMN TO THE BLESSED VIRGIN MARY"

*The angel Gabriel was sent from God to a city of Galilee named Nazareth, to a virgin betrothed to a man whose name was Joseph, of the house of David; and the virgin's name was Mary. And he came to her and said, "Hail, full of grace, the Lord is with you!"*

LUKE 1:26–28

## TODAY'S MEDITATION

Why does the Catholic Church venerate the Blessed Virgin Mary above all the other saints? Because she alone was sinless and perfectly holy. She is our model of holiness.

## PRAYER

*Good Jesus, may there never be a day when I do not praise your Blessed Mother or fail to place myself under her loving protection. Holy Mary, pray for me always.*

*St. Cuchumneus, and all you mystic saints of Ireland, pray for me!*

## Come, Holy Spirit

May the Holy Spirit be around us
Be in us and be with us:
May the Holy Spirit come to us,
O Christ, forthwith.

From demons, from sins,
From hell with all its evils:
O Jesus, may thy Spirit
Sanctify us, save us.

ST. MOLAISE (DIED C. 639),
"PRAYER TO THE HOLY SPIRIT"

*When thou sendest forth thy Spirit, they are created;*
*and thou renewest the face of the ground.*

PSALM 104:30

## Today's Meditation

We all pray to God the Father and God the Son, but the Holy Spirit rarely is the focus of prayer for most Catholics. Yet he offers us so many gifts: he will inspire us, as he inspired the authors of the Bible; he will strengthen our faith as he gave courage to Our Lady and the disciples at the first Pentecost; he came to us in a special way at our Baptism and Confirmation, and is always ready to renew those gifts.

## Prayer

*Come Holy Spirit, fill the hearts of your faithful and kindle in them the fire of your love. Send forth your Spirit and they shall be created. And You shall renew the face of the earth.*

*O, God, who by the light of the Holy Spirit, did instruct the hearts of the faithful, grant that by the same Holy Spirit we may be truly wise and ever enjoy His consolations, Through Christ Our Lord, Amen.*

*St. Molaise, and all you mystic saints of Ireland, pray for me!*

## The Ultimate Mystery

I arise today
Through a mighty strength, the invocation of the
Trinity,
Through a belief in the Threeness,
Through a confession of the Oneness
Of the Creator of creation.

ST. PATRICK, "THE BREASTPLATE," OR LORICA

*When the Counselor comes, whom I shall send to you from the Father, even the Spirit of truth, who proceeds from the Father, he will bear witness to me; and you also are witnesses, because you have been with me from the beginning.*

JOHN 15:26–27

## TODAY'S MEDITATION

The history of salvation is also the history of how God the Father, the Son, and the Holy Spirit have revealed themselves to the world. The Trinity existed before all creation, they will exist after the end of time. How that may be is incomprehensible to us, but it is enough for us to believe in the Trinity and adore the Father, the Son, and the Holy Spirit.

## PRAYER

*Glory be to the Father, and to the Son, and to the Holy Spirit. As it was in the beginning, is now, and ever shall be, world without end. Amen.*

*St. Patrick, and all you mystic saints of Ireland, pray for me!*

# The Saints

**St. Aengus the Culdee** (died c. 830): Culdees were Irish monks who followed an especially rigorous life of prayer and penance. The word "culdee" comes from the Gaelic term, *Ceile Dé*, which means "companion of God." Aengus was a member of the royal family of Ulster in northern Ireland; he gave up his rank to become first a hermit, then a monk at Tallaght Monastery on the site of modern-day Dublin. He prayed the entire psalter—150 psalms—every day. It is said that Aengus was so pure and so holy that angels came down from Heaven to converse with him. He was a gifted poet who wrote hymns in honor of the saints. Aengus also compiled the first calendar of Irish saints. Feast day: March 11.

**St. Brigid** (c. 450–525): After the Blessed Virgin Mary, St. Brigid is the most beloved female saint in Ireland. It is said that on the day Brigid was born, three angels, vested as priests, came down from Heaven to baptize her. She founded a convent at Kildare where she opened the first Christian school in Ireland. She is said to have healed lepers and madmen, restored sight to the blind and speech to the mute. The Irish loved miracle stories, and the miracles attributed to St. Brigid are especially memorable. When she was a baby, she turned water into the finest ale to quench the thirst of her nurse. When she was a girl, she was in the kitchen cooking bacon for some houseguests when a starving dog came to the door, Brigid gave all the bacon to the dog, but a moment later, when her father entered the kitchen to see if the bacon was ready, he found the frying pan overflowing with perfectly fried bacon. When Brigid was abbess of Kildare, she confronted a woman who falsely accused one of St. Patrick's disciples of fathering her child. Brigid made the Sign of the Cross over the infant and immediately the baby named his true father. St. Brigid is venerated as the patron saint of dairy workers because it is said that at her convent, the cows gave a lake of milk every day.

Feast day: February 1.


**St. Colman of Cloyne** (c. 522–600): Colman was a poet from Cork who became the bard of the king of Munster. We do not know much about his early life, but according to tradition, as a middle-aged man he met St. Brendan. This encounter inspired Colman to become a monk. On a limestone ridge in the midst of a fertile valley in County Cork, he founded a church and a monastery. Later Colman was consecrated the first bishop of the Diocese of Cloyne.

Feast day: November 24.

**St. Columba** (c. 521–597): St. Patrick, St. Brigid, and St. Columba are the three most important Irish saints, and all three are buried together in the same grave at Downpatrick, Northern Ireland. Columba was an avid collector of beautiful books. When St. Finnian, abbot of Clonnard Abbey, returned from Rome with an exquisite copy of the Psalms, Columba surreptitiously made an exact copy. When Finnian learned of the unauthorized copy, he demanded that Columba hand it over; Columba refused. The two monks appealed the case to the High King of Ireland, who settled it in Finnian's favor. Then Columba rallied his clan and waged war on Finnian and his clan. In a battle near a mountain called Ben Bulben, three thousand men were slain. Outraged by such slaughter over a book, the bishops and abbots of Ireland banished Columba for life.

With a handful of companions he sailed for Scotland, landing on the island of Iona, where they founded a monastery. Then Columba traveled to the mainland as a missionary, determined to convert one man for every man killed in his war.

Feast day: June 9.

**St. Columbanus** (c. 543–615): Many Irish monks were great wanderers, and one of the most renowned of these footloose monks was St. Columbanus. He was born into a noble family, received a fine education, and grew up to be a very handsome man. He liked the easy life his wealth and status brought him, and he enjoyed being sought-after by beautiful women. But on the advice of a female hermit, Columbanus abandoned his comfortable life and became a monk. In middle age he decided to become a missionary to the barbarian nations of Western Europe, teaching them the faith, founding monasteries among them, and opening schools where the converts' children were taught the Catholic faith as well as the Greek and Roman classics. He traveled from Ireland to England, then on to what is now Belgium, France, Germany, and Switzerland, before settling at last at Bobbio in northern Italy. St. Columbanus is often depicted with a bear, a reference to a story that once, when his monks needed help in the fields, Columbanus summoned a bear from the forest and yoked him to a plough. Feast day: November 23.

**St. Cuchumneus** (died c. 745): We know almost nothing about this saint except his name and that he wrote a life of St. Patrick as well as a celebrated hymn in honor of the Blessed Mother.

**Abbot Donogh Mór O'Daly** (died 1244): The superior of Boyle Abbey, a house of Cistercian monks in County Roscommon, Donogh Mór O'Daly was a gifted poet. About thirty of his poems have come down to us, all written in Latin.

**St. Ita** (c. 475–570): Ita was abbess of a convent at Killeedy in County Limerick. She and her nuns operated a school for boys; among their pupils was St. Brendan, the navigator-monk who is said to have sailed across the Atlantic and discovered America centuries before Christopher Columbus. She described her curriculum as, "Faith in God with purity of heart; simplicity of life with religion; generosity with love." During her life Ita was revered for her wisdom and gentle character, and it was said that she possessed the gift of prophecy, and on one famous occasion brought back to life her brother-in-law, who had been killed in battle. Feast day: January 15.

**St. Maelmuire O'Gorman** (died c. 1167): Maelmuire O'Gorman was a poet who became abbot of the monastery at Knock in County Mayo. One of his major works was a new calendar of the saints, with many more entries than the calendar compiled centuries earlier by St. Aengus the Culdee. Maelmuire said that he hoped all Christians who chanted the entries would, through the intercession of all the saints, be granted eternal salvation.

Feast day: July 3.

**St. Molaise** (died c. 639): As a young man Molaise left Ireland to live as a hermit on Holy Isle, off the coast of Scotland. Several years later he made a pilgrimage to Rome. While there, he may have been consecrated a bishop. He returned to Ireland, where he entered the monastery at Old Leighlin in County Carlow. The Church in Ireland followed a different liturgical calendar and lived a different style of monastic life than the Church elsewhere in Europe; Molaise tried very gently to persuade his monks to follow the Roman liturgical calendar, and adopt the monastic rule of St. Benedict. It is not known how successful he was in this. In addition to serving as abbot, Molaise wrote works of poetry and prose, a few of which have survived.

Feast day: April 18.

**St. Patrick** (c. 387–c. 464): About the year 403, when Patrick was sixteen years old, Irish raiders kidnapped him from his home in Britain and sold him into slavery in Ireland. Although his parents were Catholic (his father was a deacon), by the time he was in his early teens Patrick had become an atheist. In his autobiography, the Confession, he admits candidly, "I did not believe in the living God." But in Ireland, a poorly clothed, under-fed slave, he turned back to God. After six years of slavery he received a message from heaven that it was time to escape. He ran to the coast, found a ship, and persuaded the crew to take him aboard.

He was back his with family when one night he had a dream in which a stranger presented him with a piece of paper that bore the inscription, "The Voice of the Irish." Then he heard countless Irish voices crying out to him, "We beg you, holy youth, come and walk among us once more." Soon thereafter Patrick traveled to Gaul (modern-day France), to study for the priesthood.

We do not know the exact year Patrick made his missionary journey to Ireland. Certainly he was there by 450. He traveled extensively in the provinces of Ulster, Leinster, and Munster, where he made enormous numbers of converts. The Irish responded enthusiastically to the Catholic faith, and many young men and young women asked to be received as monks or nuns. Since St. Patrick's day, Irish missionary priests, nuns, and brothers have carried Catholicism to every corner of the globe. According to tradition, St. Patrick drove all the snakes out of Ireland. It is true that there are no serpents in Ireland, but a Roman visitor noticed this phenomenon centuries before Patrick arrived. The legend is taken as a metaphor for the pagan religion that Patrick swept away.

Feast day: March 17.

**St. Sechnall** (c. 372–457): Sechnall was the son of St. Patrick's sister, Liamain; he was one of nine brothers, eight of whom entered the priesthood and became bishops in Ireland. Like his uncle, he studied for the priesthood in Gaul. In 432, when the pope sent Patrick to Ireland as a missionary bishop, Sechnall accompanied him. Patrick consecrated Sechnall first bishop of Dunshaughlin in County Meath. His congregation of newly converted Irish was large, but they had not entirely absorbed the finer points of Catholicism. For example, they moved the annual fair from the open fields into the enclosed churchyard of Sechnall's cathedral. When he rebuked them for having no respect for consecrated ground, the crowd ignored him. It's said that God showed His displeasure by splitting open the ground, which swallowed up thirteen horses, chariots, and charioteers. St. Sechnall's poem recounting the life of St. Patrick is the first Latin poem composed in Ireland. His hymn in honor of the Blessed Sacrament, "Sanct venite," is still sung in the British Isles. According to legend, Sechnall didn't really compose it, he just wrote down what he heard angels singing.

Feast day: November 27.

## About the Author

For the last 30 years, Thomas Craughwell has been an independent scholar of the saints, digging through the autobiographies and letters of the saints, as well the writings of their contemporaries, to get past the sentimentality that tends to surround saints and find the living, breathing, struggling, real-life men and women.

Craughwell is a full-time freelance writer. Among his published works are the highly acclaimed *Saints Behaving Badly* (Doubleday, 2006), *Saints for Every Occasion* (Stampley, 2001), and *Saints Preserved: An Encyclopedia of Relics* (Image, 2011). He has written more than two dozen books on history, religion, and popular culture.

Craughwell has written about saints for *Wall Street Journal*, *American Spectator*, *Inside the Vatican*, *National Catholic Register*, and many Catholic publications. He is a regular contributor to *Our Sunday Visitor*, and writes a monthly column on patron saints for diocesan newspapers.

A popular speaker, Craughwell has appeared on EWTN, CNN, Discovery Channel and more than 150 radio stations to discuss saints, the canonization process, and Catholic history. He was also featured in The History Channel adaptation of one of his highly praised historical books, *Stealing Lincoln's Body*.

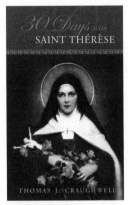
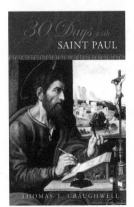